A Tucker and Zoey Adventure
The Bone War

SECOND EDITION
Copyright © 2024

Written by Christian Bensing 🐾 Illustrated by Timothy Feather

All rights reserved. No part of this book without written consent by the author may be used or reproduced in any way except in critical articles or reviews.

Contact the publisher for information.
Paperback ISBN: 978-1-7330791-1-2
Hardcover ISBN: 978-1-7330791-0-5

Tucker and Zoey Adventures 🐾 P.O. Box 195, Springtown, PA 18081
tuckerandzoeyadventures.com

This book is dedicated to all the rescues out there.
If humans had even a fraction of your love,
spirit, optimism, and heart, the world
would be a better place. You give
us more than we ever deserve.

Daydreaming in his comfy bed,
Memories danced inside Tucker's head.
His days as a puppy were now long in the past,
And his life had changed so remarkably fast.

He was a handsome dog covered
In wrinkles and dimples
Whose dream for the future
Was really quite simple:
Food in his tummy,
A warm loving home,
Soft pats on the head,
Belly rubs, and a bone.

But he lived in a foster home with dogs so tall,
It was like he did not even exist at all.
They pushed and they trampled, butted and slobbered,
Wagged baseball bat tails, and poor Tucker got clobbered!

At dinner he sat back while the other dogs begged
And looked on through a forest of giant dog legs.
Only after they finished would he get to eat.
The leftover water smelled like dirty dog feet!

To make things worse, after all the dogs had been fed,
Tasty chewable bones were laid out before bed.
To chew one so yummy, Tuck knew he deserved;
But it was always a case of first come, first served.

With the big dogs around Tucker had no shot
To savor a bone, no matter how hard he fought.
Then some good news came that would change Tucker's life.
He was adopted by a man and his beautiful wife!

Now he had room to roam in a green, grassy yard!
There were no other dogs, and he was the star!
Tucker finally found a place to call home
With a bed, food and water, plus his very own bone.

Tuck was in heaven, the world's luckiest dog.
He would play all day long and then sleep like a log.
He was king of the dog park with oodles of friends,
But Tucker's life soon would be changing again.

He was chasing a butterfly
In the back yard
When Tuck heard his people
Get out of their car.
They walked through the gate,
But they were not alone.
Something on four legs had
Followed them home.

It wore a pink dress, but it looked like a twig!
And Tucker had never seen ears quite so big!
It shivered and shook with bright, googly eyes.
Then the man said to Tucker, "This is Zoey – surprise!"

This can't be a dog, was the thought in his head.
He wanted to growl but then sniffed her instead.
Annoyed and suspicious, he tried to be nice.
Zoey flashed her teeth and snarled at him twice!

It caught Tuck off guard – how dare she be mean!
Threatened by a dog that looked like a string bean!
Tucker barked with fury. Zoey shivered and groaned.
He would ignore this pipsqueak and go chew his bone.

The dogs kept their distance for the next few days.
Zoey did her best to stay out of Tuck's way.
Till one day she peeked out and saw Tucker chewing.
She came out of hiding to see what he was doing.

Closer and closer she inched and she sneaked,
Anxious to get just the tiniest peek.
What was it that Tucker so treasured and savored,
All coated with slobber and bursting with flavor?

Zoey licked her lips, eyes wide with wonder,
Ready to strike like lightning and thunder.
The bone was right there, only two feet away –
Smelly, slimy, and perfect in every way.

Tucker saw Zoey from the corner of his eye.
He picked up the bone, and he held it up high.
No one was stealing his highly-prized treasure.
To deny this runt would be his pleasure!

He turned his back and looked over his shoulder,
Sensing the chihuahua was getting much bolder.
He marched out of the room and took with him the bone
Until he heard ringing, a call on the phone!

Dogs sprint and bark when they hear a loud noise,
So Tuck darted past furniture, sneakers, and toys.
But by the time he got there, the ringing had stopped,
And that's when he realized his bone he had dropped!

His forehead wrinkled with fear and worry.
Rolls of skin 'round his eyes made his vision blurry.
Tuck bolted faster than any jet could have flown,
But he was too late. Zoey captured the bone!

Tucker could not believe then and there what he saw.
That little thief had the bone in her paws!
She chewed it so wildly, he heard her lips smack
With no intentions of giving it back.

Tucker stomped his feet and stood up tall,
But the chihuahua did not seem to care, not at all!
The glistening glow from her oversized peepers
Made it quite clear - FINDERS KEEPERS!

Zoey wanted Tucker to leave her alone.
She high-tailed it out of there, dragging the bone.
But the bone was so heavy for a canine so small
That she dropped it before getting too far at all.

Tucker pounced when he saw the bone on the floor.
This was an honest-to-goodness bone war!
Zoey was tiny, but Tuck did not care.
She had left it behind. It was his, fair and square!

That is what Tuck thought, but he was not so sure
When right by him flashed a black and white blur.
The chihuahua again! She was on the attack!
Zoey had the bone once and was taking it back!

There was no way Zoey would be denied.
She had visions of whisking it somewhere outside.
But the wife scooped her up, held her high in the air –
Zoey was up here, and the bone was down there!

With a smile on his mug, Tucker watched with glee
As the wife spoke baby talk to her "sweet little chi."
Zoey squirmed, and she fought off the snuggles and hugs.
Tucker dashed with the bone, burning out on the rug!

He ripped through the screen door with a thunderous crash
Like a thief on the run with a big bag of cash.
To a dog a bone is worth much more than money,
And Tuck was home free… until he felt something funny.

It was a feeling a dog hates more than trips to the vet,
And he knew this would be the very worst yet.
His entire body began to twitch.
A dog's worst nightmare, an unreachable itch!

Tucker stopped in his tracks and flopped onto his back.
The only thing on his mind was a much-needed scratch.
He wriggled and squirmed. Grass flew all around!
But so did the bone, right onto the ground.

By that time Zoey was back on the scene.
She zipped out the door through the hole in the screen.
With Tuck on the ground and the bone in clear sight,
Zoey snatched it up and quickly took flight.

She ran faster than a greyhound or any gazelle,
With the bone in her jaws, fully under its spell.
Zoey found a good spot behind the old shed
And gnawed on the bone like she had never been fed.

All alone at last, Zoey's dream come true!
Now there was nothing that Tucker could do!
She would finish the bone while he tried to regroup,
But her joy turned to panic – she had to poop!

Zoey laid the bone down, dejected and defeated,
Took care of her business, then sadly retreated.
There was never a doubt that she gave it her all,
But you never quite know when nature will call.

The bone war was over, and Tuck had prevailed.
He pranced like a champion and wagged his proud tail.
Zoey proved a great challenge, but he was the ace.
Now he wanted to rub it in that little runt's face!

Bone held high, Tucker trotted indoors.
There he found Zoey curled up on the floor.
Her eyes were welled up with buckets of tears,
And Tuck's feeling of triumph at once disappeared.

In his heart was a feeling he could not quite place
Until he saw HIMSELF in that little girl's face.
Hers was a look that was once his own
Before he was adopted into his wonderful home.

The wife sat down and held Zoey near
While the man rubbed Tucker behind his right ear.
His golden-brown eyes peeked from under his brow
As the man shared with him Zoey's story till now.

"She was the runt of twelve dogs
And had no one who cared.
She lived every day nervous,
Worried and scared.
We brought her home from that
Unpleasant place
To a strong, brave brother
Who can keep her safe."

The man patted Tuck's head,
And it all became clear.
There was a reason both he
And Zoey were here.
She was now his sister,
And he was her brother.
Together as family,
They needed each other..

Tucker glimpsed in her eyes, and he knew this was true.
There was something special that he had to do.
His face became wrinkled with guilt and regret.
He nudged Zoey the bone with his nose, black and wet.

He cuddled up close and gave her a snuggle.
Zoey planted a kiss on his warm, fuzzy muzzle.
Two dogs so different with similar pasts
Together found a forever family, at last.

Gazing up at his people, Tucker saw their proud smiles.
Now the bone war seemed silly and hardly worthwhile.
Zoey was not an intruder but a sibling instead,
Who quickly decided... to steal Tucker's bed!

Printed in the USA
CPSIA information can be obtained
at www.ICGtesting.com
LVHW061429270324
775236LV00002B/3